Rachel Garton is a practicing solicitor at Gosschalks LLP, specialising in property dispute resolution.

Her work comprises of all areas of property litigation and landlord and tenant matters including: residential long leasehold, tenants right of first refusal, lease renewal litigation, commercial and residential possession proceedings, residential and commercial service charge disputes and debt recovery.

She has a niche specialism in assured shorthold tenancies and has delivered a number of seminars for MBL Seminars on topics related to this subject such as asbestos in residential properties, tenancy deposits in flat shares and the upcoming Renter's Reform Bill.

A Practical Guide to Tenancy Deposits in Assured Shorthold Tenancies

A Practical Guide to Tenancy Deposits in Assured Shorthold Tenancies

Rachel Garton
BSC (Hons), LL.Dip, LL.PgDip

Law Brief Publishing

Published 2022 by Law Brief Publishing, an imprint of Law Brief Publishing Ltd
30 The Parks
Minehead
Somerset
TA24 8BT

www.lawbriefpublishing.com

Paperback: 978-1-914608-23-0

To Byron, Lilah, Sawyer, Ethan,
Jacob, Ethan and Ember

PREFACE

With the number of tenancy deposit disputes rising, this work is intended to serve as a simple guide to the key issues for practitioners. Each chapter provides insight into points that commonly arise and aims to provide the guidance necessary to advise on how to deal with tenancy deposits in assured shorthold tenancies as well as assist with tenancy deposit disputes.

This book endeavours to summarise the current law on tenancy deposits in assured shorthold tenancies as of 31 March 2022. It firstly deals with the relevant legislation, how and when it complies and the sanctions for non-compliance. It ends by dealing with particular scenarios that may arise and upcoming changes in the legislation.

Rachel Garton
May 2022

CONTENTS

CHAPTER ONE

THE LEGISLATION

Introduction

The Housing Act 2004 ('HA 2004') introduced new legislation in respect of how landlords must deal with tenancy deposits that are received when granting an assured shorthold tenancy ('AST'). The legislation has been subsequently amended by the Localism Act 2011 ('LA 2011') and the Deregulation Act 2015 ('DA 2015') to provide further clarification on the landlord's requirements when dealing with deposits and also to introduce further requirements and restrictions. It is crucial for landlords to be aware of the legislation to ensure compliance. This chapter aims to provide a summary of the current legislative framework.

HA 2004

The rules relating to tenancy deposits in respect of ASTs were introduced by the HA 2004 and came into force on 6 April 2007. Since this date when a deposit is received from the tenant on the commencement of an AST a landlord must:

(a) join a Tenancy Deposit Scheme ('TDS') ;

(b) pay the deposit into the TDS;

(c) Comply with the initial requirements of the TDS ;

(d) Serve prescribed information on the tenant.

The requirements set out above were to be complied with within 14 days of receiving the deposit. This has now been extended 30 days for those deposits taken on or after 6 April 2012 as discussed below.

The intention of the legislation was to ensure that landlords returned deposits to tenants at the end of the AST, where payable and also to allow landlords to have a sum of money to cover any or a proportion of the rent/damages due at the end of the AST, if any.

The above obligations in the HA 2004 only apply to ASTs and the landlord and tenant cannot contract out of the above obligations.

The HA 2004 has been subsequently amended by section 184 of the LA 2011 on 6 April 2012 and on 26 March 2015 by sections 30- 40 of the DA 2015.The amendments are discussed below.

A summary of the relevant sections of the HA 2004 are below. These will be covered in more detail throughout this book.

Section 212 of the HA 2004

Section 212 provides a definition of a TDS as:

(a) made for the purpose of safeguarding tenancy deposits paid in connection with ASTs and facilitating the resolution of disputes arising in connection with such deposits, and

(b) complies with the requirements of Schedule 10 of the HA 2004.

Section 212 also makes provision for financial assistance to be offered to scheme administrators.

Section 213 of the HA 2004

Section 213 contains provisions on:

(a) when landlords must join a TDS

(b) the requirements in relation to prescribed information

(c) preventing the parties from contracting out of the requirements.

Section 214 of the HA 2004

Section 214 contains the provisions in relation to the tenant making applications to the Court if the landlord has not complied with the requirements.

Section 215 of the HA 2004

Section 215 contains provisions on the sanctions imposed on landlords for non-compliance.

Schedule 10 of the HA 2004

Schedule 10 contains provisions relating to:

- The types of TDS.
- The termination of tenancies.
- Notification to tenants of any requests made to the scheme administrator.
- Dispute resolution.

- Service of documents.
- The power of the appropriate national authority to amend Schedule 10.
- Interpretation.

Section 184 of the LA 2011

The HA 2004 did not set out any sanctions for the landlord's failure to comply with the legislation. As a result, some landlords were simply not complying with the requirements and deposits were not being returned to tenants at the end of ASTS. In addition, those landlords who were trying to comply with the legislation, were struggling to register deposits received within the allocated 14 days.

To deal with these issues the LA 2011 amended sections 213 to 215 of the HA 2004 as follows:

- It introduced a penalty to landlords for failing to comply with the HA 2004. If the landlord failed to register the deposit in a TDS and comply with the requirements of that TDS, the tenant was entitled to compensation in the sum of one to three times the amount of the deposit they had paid. The penalty applies even if the landlord has simply been late complying with the legislation.
- It introduced a further sanction on landlords by stating that if the deposit is not protected in a TDS, the landlord will only be able to serve a notice pursuant to section 21 of the Housing Act 1988 ('HA 1988') once the landlord has rectified the breach by repaying the deposit or following determination, settlement or withdrawal of any claim.
- It extended the right of the tenant to apply to the Court in respect

of compliance so that it applied even if the AST has ended.

- It extended the time for the landlord to pay the deposit into a TDS and serve the prescribed information on the tenant from 14 to 30 days.

Article 16 of the LA 2011 provided that the changes introduced by section 184 of the LA 2011 only applied to deposits received on or after 6 April 2012 and that the changes did not apply if the landlord had complied with the initial requirements of the TDS and given the prescribed information within 30 days from 6 April 2012 i.e. by 6 May 2012.

Sections 30-40 of the DA 2015

As a result of the provisions introduced by the LA 2011, lots of questions arose as to how the legislation applied in certain scenarios. On 26 March 2015, the DA 2015 sought to address some of the queries by making the following amendments to the legislation:

- If there was a fixed term AST entered into before 6 April 2007 where the landlord took a deposit, that became a periodic tenancy after 6 April 2007 and was still in existence on 26 March 2015, the landlord was given 90 days from 26 March 2015 to register the deposit.

- If the landlord took a deposit after 6 April 2007 and complied with the requirements the landlord's compliance would suffice if that AST became, or becomes, a statutory periodic tenancy.

- If the landlord received a deposit before 6 April 2007 and the AST became periodic before 6 April 2007 there is no financial penalty for failure to register the deposit.

- It is acceptable to give the details of the landlord's agent, in the Prescribed Information, if the agent protected the deposit at the outset of the AST.

These scenarios as well as further scenarios are discussed in chapter 6.

The Tenants Fees Act 2019 ('TFA 2019')

On 1 June 2019, the TFA 2019 came into force which introduced further protection for tenants of ASTS as it sets out a number of payments that landlords or agents were now prohibited from taking from tenants. In respect of deposits, paragraph 2 of Schedule 1 of TFA 2019 capped the amount that can be taken as a deposit to:

(a) 5 weeks rent where the annual rent under the AST is less than £50,000.00;

(b) 6 weeks rent where the annual rent under the AST is more than £50,000.00.

If a landlord accepts a deposit from a tenant above the caps set out it will be a prohibited payment under the TFA 2019, and the landlord will be expected to return the deposit. The landlord will not be able to serve a notice requiring possession under section 21 of the HA 1988 until they have returned the deposit to the tenant and may also be subject to a financial penalty.

The cap is based on the amount of the rent at the point of the grant, renewal, or continuance of the AST. Therefore, if the parties agree to reduce the rent part way through the term of an existing AST, there will be no need to reduce the amount of the deposit held. If, however, the parties agree to a new or renewal AST with a lower rent, the amount of the deposit would need to be reduced and part of the deposit returned to the tenant.

Summary

The HA 2004 introduced legislation on how deposits should be dealt with by landlords. There has been a number of amendments to the HA 2004 and the provisions relating to

deposits since the HA 2004 was introduced to try and address some issues that arose from its implementation. It is vital that landlords are aware of their requirements, so they do not fall foul of the legislation and face sanctions as a result.

CHAPTER TWO

WHEN DOES THE LEGISLATION SET OUT IN THE HA 2004 (AS AMENDED) APPLY?

Introduction

The legislation in the HA 2004 (as amended) only apply to ASTs and to rent deposits that are received in respect of an AST. This chapter aims to set out what qualifies as an AST and what is likely to constitute a deposit.

What is an AST?

Any tenancy entered into on or after 28 February 1997 will be an AST if it qualifies as an assured tenancy under Section 1 of the HA 1988. Section 1 of the HA 1988 states the following is an assured tenancy:

> *"A tenancy under which a dwelling-house is let as a separate dwelling is for the purposes of this Act an assured tenancy id and so long as-*
>
> *(a) The tenant or, as the case may be, each of the joint tenants is an individual: and*
>
> *(b) The tenant or, as the case may be, at least one of the joint tenants occupies the dwelling house as his only or principal home; and*

> *(c) The tenancy is not one which, by virtue of subsection (2) or subsection (6) below, cannot be an assured tenancy."*

To be an AST, the following must therefore apply:

(i) There must be a tenancy

(ii) It must be a tenancy of a dwelling-house

(iii) The dwelling-house must have been let as a separate dwelling

(iv) The tenant must be an individual. The tenant cannot be a company.

(v) The tenant must occupy the dwelling-house as their only or principal home

A tenancy will not be an AST if even if it satisfies the above requirements if the tenancy is one of the exceptions listed in schedule 1 of the HA 1988. These exceptions are as follows:

(i) Tenancies created before 15 January 1989, or a tenancy entered into pursuant to a contract made before that date (paragraph 1, schedule 1 HA 1988)

(ii) Tenancies of high value properties. A high value property is as follows:

(a) If the tenancy is post 1 April 1990 – a property with an annual rent more that £100,000. (paragraph 2, schedule 1 HA 1988)

(b) If the tenancy is pre-1 April 1990 – a property with a rateable value over £750.00 or £1,500.00 in greater London (paragraph 2A, schedule 1 HA 1988)

(iii) Tenancies at a low rent. A low rent is as follow:

(a) A tenancy where no rent is payable (paragraph 3, Schedule 1 HA 1988)

(b) If the tenancy is post 1 April 1990 – the annual rent payable is less that £250.00 per annum or less that £1,000.00 in greater London(paragraph 3A, schedule 1 HA 1988)

(c) If the tenancy is pre-1 April 1990 – the annual rent payable is less than 2 thirds of the rateable value of the property on 31 March 1990 (paragraph 3B, schedule 1 HA 1988)

(iv) Business tenancies to which the Landlord and Tenant Act 1954 applies. (paragraph 4, schedule 1 HA 1988)

(v) Licensed Premises – tenancies that are licensed for the sale of intoxicating liquors for consumption on the premises (paragraph 5, schedule 1 HA 1988).

(vi) Tenancies where agricultural land of more than 2 acres is let with a dwelling house and tenancies of agricultural holdings or farm business tenancies (paragraph 6 and 7, schedule 1 HA 1988)

(vii) Student lettings by certain landlords (paragraph 8, schedule 1 HA 1988)

(viii) Holiday lettings (paragraph 9, Schedule 1 HA 1988)

(ix) Lettings by resident landlords (paragraph 10, schedule 1 HA 1988)

(x) Crown tenancies. These are tenancies where the interest of the landlord belongs to or is held in trust for Her Majesty in the right of the Crown or to a government department (Paragraph 11, schedule 1 HA 1988).

(xi) Local Authority tenancies (paragraph 12, schedule 1 HA 1988).

(xii) Family intervention tenancies (paragraph 12ZA, schedule 1 HA 1988)

The author is not going to go into great detail on the exceptions above. However. If it is believed a tenancy may fall under any of the exceptions, it is advised that a review of the relevant paragraph of the Schedule 1 takes place to check the finer details.

A tenancy entered into before 28 February 1997 will also be an AST if:

(i) it qualifies as an assured tenancy under Section 1 of the HA 1988 (see above) and;

(ii) it is for a fixed term. The fixed term has to be a minimum of 6 months but there is no upper limit to the term, and;

(iii) a notice was served by the landlord on the tenant pursuant to section 20 of the HA 1988 prior to entering into the tenancy stating the tenancy is an AST.

If a tenancy entered into before 28 February 1997 does not satisfy the above criteria it is likely to be an assured tenancy not an AST.

What is a Deposit?

Typically, a deposit is a lump sum that a tenant will pay to the landlord on the outset of a tenancy and prior to being allowed into the property. The deposit is then held until the end of the tenancy with a view to it either being returned to the tenant when they vacate or being retained by the landlord if the tenant is in breach of the tenancy and the landlord has a claim for sums due as a result. ASTs commonly contain a provision requiring the tenant to pay a deposit.

Section 212(8) of the Housing Act 2004 defines a tenancy deposit in relation to an AST as:-

"Any money intended to be held (by the landlord or otherwise) as security for:-

(a) The performance of any obligations of the tenant; or

(b) The discharge of any liability of his, arising under or in connection with the tenancy."

It is important to note that a deposit does not necessarily have to be a lump sum taken at the outset and referred to as a 'deposit' in the AST. Any sum paid by the tenant to the landlord which is effectively being held with a view to being retained if the tenant is in default of their liabilities may be seen as a deposit. Some examples of sums taken that are likely to be deemed as deposits are:

(a) Additional money charged as rent each month which is collected from the tenant by the landlord with an intention to be offset against potential rent arrears or the costs of cleaning and repairs.

(b) A cleaning fee which is paid by the tenant to the landlord in advance and is to be repaid to the tenant at the end of the AST if the tenant has left the property clean in accordance with the AST and the cleaning fee is not required.

Even if there is a clear provision in the AST for a cleaning fee or an additional fee to be repaid to the tenant at the end of the term it can still be deemed to be a deposit.

A further question that has arisen in the use of ASTs since the introduction of the HA 2004 is whether a rent advance can or will constitute a deposit. This is not straight forward but it has been held that rent advances can constitute a deposit. There is a difference between money paid to the landlord to discharge an existing obligation and money paid to the landlord as security for such an obligation. If the payment is genuinely in advance of rent and the landlord or the agent is using the payment to offset against the rent the payment is unlikely to be held to be a rent deposit. If, however, the landlord has taken a payment from the tenant and called it a rent advance but is in fact holding it in case of tenant's breach, it is effectively being held as security and will constitute a deposit.

Relevant Cases

Piggott v Slaven (2009)

Ms Slaven was granted an AST in 2005. At the outset he paid Mr Piggott a £600.00 deposit. Ms Slaven was then granted a new AST for a different property in 2008. Mr Piggott repaid £75.00 of the deposit to Ms Slaven but retained the remaining £525.00. Mr Piggott stated this was in respect of the first weeks rent of £105.00 and the remaining £420.00 was rent in advance.

The landlord served a notice under section 21 of the HA 1988 and the Court had to assess whether the sums retained by the Mr Piggott amounted to a deposit in order to determine if Mr Piggott was entitled to possession.

In determining whether the £505.00 retained was a deposit the Judge referred to section 212 (8) of the HA 2004 and held that whether or not the money retained amounted to security should be assessed objectively. It was held that any money kept over the first weeks rent which in this case was the additional £420.00 was clearly being held as security in the event that Ms Slaven failed to pay the rent due under the AST. Mr Piggott had not offset the money retained against the first 5 weeks rent. The fact the sums taken amounted to a deposit cannot be avoided simply by a landlord stating that it is not a deposit or being held as a security if factually that is exactly what is being done.

Further information on the consequences of non- compliance with the legislation and obtaining possession under section 21 of the HA 1988 is at Chapter 6.

Johnson & Others -v- Old [2013]

Mrs Old entered into an AST dated 1 May 2009 for a fixed term of 6 months. At the outset she paid a deposit of £1,425.00 to the landlord's agent and a sum equivalent to six months' rent. The deposit of £1425,00.00 was paid into a TDS. The sum received for 6 months' rent in advance was to be used by the landlord's agent against the rent due each month and the agent did pay a sum equivalent to one month's rent to the landlord, Mr Johnson each month from the rent advance received.

The AST dated 1 May 2009 expired and Mrs Old entered into a new AST which again included the payment of the deposit of £1,425.00 as well as the payment of a sum equivalent to 6 months' rent. When the second AST expired a third AST was entered into on similar terms to the previous 2 ASTs with the exception that the rent was increased. The rent now amounted to £1,000.00 per month so Mrs Old was required to pay £6000.00 upfront by way of a 6 months' rent advance on the commencement of the third AST. The third AST expired on 31 October 2010 but this time the tenant held over under statutory periodic tenancy. The sums paid in advance on the outset of the third AST had been allocated to the rent due in the fixed term of the third AST.

Mrs Old fell into arrears in respect of the statutory periodic tenancy that arose on the expiry of the third AST. On 14 August 2011 Mr Johnson served a notice under section 21 of the HA 1988 requiring possession of the property. The Court had to decide if the 6 months' rent advance taken by Mr Johnson amounted to a rent deposit as if so, he was in breach of the legislation as he has failed to register the deposit in a TDS.

In the first instance, it was held that the rent advance had been paid in security and amounted to a rent deposit and the possession proceedings under Section 21 of the HA 1988 were dismissed due to his failure to register the deposit in a TDS.

Mr Johnson appealed and the Judge on appeal held that the £6000.00 taken did amount to a rent advance and not security for the obligation to pay rent. The Judge stated that there is a difference in money paid to discharge an existing obligation and money paid as security for such an obligation. The Court of Appeal raised the hypothetical question of having paid £6,000.00 in advance, how Mrs Old would have reacted if she had then been asked to pay rent in the initial fixed term of the third AST. The Court concluded that it was likely that Mrs Old would have said she was not paying the rent requested as she had paid the first 6 months in advance at the outset of the AST. This was further supported by the provisions of the AST and the agents conduct in allocating the payments.

The Court also addressed the fact that a new periodic tenancy had been formed when the third AST came to an end and that no payment and/or had been taken in respect of this new tenancy. The creation of new tenancies and the requirements in relation to deposits is discussed in chapter 6.

As there was no deposit, Mr Johnson was not in breach of the legislation and was entitled to possession under section 21 of the HA 1988.

The decision in this case was welcomed by landlords as prior to this finding landlord had been concerned that in light of the decision of *Piggott v Slaven* that any money taken in advance of rent would constitute a deposit

A deposit consisting of property

Under section 213 (7) of the HA 2004 a landlord cannot require a deposit which consists of property other than money.

Summary

Landlords need to firstly be careful that they recognise if they have granted an AST to a tenant ore tenants and secondly that if any money taken in respect of the AST amounts to a deposit, they follow the legislation and protect the deposit. Despite the case of *Johnson & Others v Old*, landlords still need to be careful in light of Piggott and ensure they do not try and disguise deposits as advance payments in respect of rent. There is always a possibility of an argument if a rent advance is taken about whether it amounts to a deposit. The costs of arguing this point may be best avoided by simply not taking a rent advance. However, if the landlord wants to do so they need to ensure the AST is clearly worded and that they do use the rent advance to offset against the rent as intended and not hold the sum as security.

CHAPTER THREE

WHAT IS A TDS?

Introduction

The HA 2004 (as amended) states that a landlord must register a tenancy deposit in respect of an AST within 30 days of receipt of the deposit. In order to comply it is necessary to be aware of what a TDS is and the types of TDS that are available. The aim of this chapter is to discuss the 2 types of TDS available and how they work with a particular focus on how each TDS deals with tenancy deposit disputes.

What is the definition of a TDS?

The HA 2004 defines a TDS as a scheme that is made for the purpose of safeguarding tenancy deposits paid in connection with ASTs, facilitates the resolution of disputes arising in connection with tenancy deposits and complies with schedule 10 to the HA 2004 (section 212 (2) of the HA 2004). Schedule 10 of the HA 2004 is dealt with in part below.

TDSs are not classed as Collective Investment Schemes. This is stated in the Financial Services and Markets Act 2000 (Collective Investment Schemes) Order 2001 (SI 2001/1062), as amended by the Financial Services and Markets Act 2000 (Collective Investment Schemes) (Amendment) Order 2007 (SI 2007/800). This is presumably because the purpose or effect of the TDS is not to enable the participants to receive profits or income out of the property.

Scheme Administrators

TDSs are maintained by scheme administrators, and it is important that landlords read the terms and conditions for their particular TDS as each TDS will have slightly different terms. One particular term to check will be in respect of the service of documents and methods of service to ensure compliance.

Types of TDS

Paragraph 1 (1) of schedule 10 states that a TDS must be either a custodial scheme or an insurance scheme.

Custodial TDS

In a custodial TDS, the landlord pays the deposit into a separate designated account in the name of the scheme administrator. The scheme administrator holds the deposit on behalf of the landlord and the tenant during the course of the AST. The deposit is not held by the landlord.

Neither the landlord nor the tenant has to pay a fee to use the scheme. The scheme is actually funded by the portion of the interest earned on the deposit while it's held by the scheme administrator.

At the end of the tenancy, the landlord and tenant can jointly ask for the deposit to be repaid and if they have agreed on the proportion to be paid to the tenant and to the landlord, the scheme administrator will pay out the sums agreed within 10 days of the notification (paragraph 4(2) and 4(3) of schedule 10)

Scheme administrators have the power to pay out the interest that has accrued on the deposit to the tenant and landlord. However, this is likely to be minimal, if anything at all due to the funding of a custodial

TDS. The provisions in relation to the payment of interest are set out at paragraph 3 of schedule 10.

If there is a dispute between the parties as to what portion of the deposit should be returned to the tenant, the TDS provides an Alternative Dispute Resolution ('ADR') service to assist the parties in reaching an agreement. If this is successful, the scheme administrator will pay out the sums in accordance with what was agreed in the ADR.

If the parties cannot agree either independently or through ADR, either party can refer the determination of who the deposit is payable to through the Court or an adjudicator. Once the split is determined the scheme administrator has to pay out the sums in accordance with the decision/order within 10 days of the notification (paragraph 4 (4) and 4(5) of Schedule 10).

One scenario that does arise is where the tenant or landlord is either absent or uncooperative. In this case how can either the tenant or the landlord receives the deposit from the TDS? Schedule 10 considers this scenario and provides provisions for the landlord to apply in these circumstances.

Landlord's Application

Where a landlord is not getting a response from a tenant in respect of the deposit there is provision that the landlord can apply to the TDS for the whole or part of the deposit to be provided to them. An application can be made if at least 14 days have passed since the AST ended, no agreement has been made with the tenant and either the landlord has no current address for the tenant or any means of contacting the tenant or the landlord has sent written notice to the tenant asking whether the tenant accepts the proposed deposit and the tenant has not responded within 14 days (paragraph 4A of schedule 10).

An absent tenant is quite a common scenario as tenants will often vacate the property and not provide a forwarding address to the landlord. Just because the landlord does not know the whereabouts of the tenant, doesn't mean the landlord is automatically entitled to the deposit. The landlord will still need to show that the deposit is payable to them and that they have a claim for the deposit due to rent arrears and/or breach of covenant such as disrepair.

A statutory declaration has to accompany the application to contain :

(a) the date on which the tenancy ended;

(b) that the landlord and the tenant have not reached any agreement under paragraph 4(2) of schedule 10 with respect to the amount claimed, with details of any communications between them since that date (whether relating to the relevant amount or otherwise);

(c) the basis on which the amount claimed is calculated, with particulars of any facts relied on to justify claiming that amount;

(d) if the landlord relies on the condition in sub-paragraph (3), that he has no current address for, or other means of contacting, the tenant, giving particulars of any address (other than the premises subject to the tenancy) and other contact details (including telephone numbers or e mail addresses) which the landlord has had for the tenant;

(e) if the landlord relies on the condition in sub-paragraph (4), that the condition is met, with particulars of the facts relied on to demonstrate that it is met and attaching a copy of the notice given to the tenant;

(f) any information the landlord has as to the whereabouts of the tenant;

(g) that the landlord gives their consent, in the event of the tenant disputing that the landlord should be paid the amount claimed, for the dispute to be resolved through the use of the dispute resolution service;

(h) that the landlord considers that they are entitled to be paid the amount claimed;

and

(i) that the landlord makes the statutory declaration knowing that if they knowingly and wilfully makes a false declaration they may be liable to prosecution under the Perjury Act 1911.

(Paragraph 4A (7) of schedule 10)

Tenant's Application

Where the landlord is absent, and the tenant wants the deposit to be returned to them there is provision for them to apply to the TDS for all or part of the deposit. Tenants are able to apply if at least 14 days have passed since the tenancy has ended, there is no agreement between the parties on payment of the deposit and either the tenant has no current address for the landlord or the tenant has no means of contacting the landlord or the tenant has served a written notice on the landlord asking for all or part of the the deposit and the landlord has not responded in 14 days (paragraph 4B of schedule 10). As with the landlord's application, the tenant has to have a genuine belief that they are entitled to the amount of the deposit claimed, i.e., there are no rent arrears etc. that would mean the landlord is entitled to all or part of the deposit. In support of the tenant's assertion that they are entitled to the all or part of the deposit their application needs to contain a statutory declaration which includes the following:

(a) the date on which the tenancy ended;

(b) that the landlord and the tenant have not reached any agreement under paragraph 4(2) with respect to the amount claimed, with details of any communications between them since that date (whether relating to the relevant amount or otherwise);

(c) if the tenant relies on the condition in sub-paragraph (3), that he has no current address for, or other means of contacting, the landlord, giving particulars of any address and other contact details (including telephone numbers or e mail addresses) which the tenant has had for the landlord;

(d) if the tenant relies on the condition in sub-paragraph (4), that the condition is met, with particulars of the facts relied on to demonstrate that it is met and attaching a copy of the notice given to the landlord;

(e) any information the tenant has as to the whereabouts of the landlord;

(f) that the tenant gives their consent, in the event of the landlord disputing that the tenant should be paid the amount claimed, for the dispute to be resolved through the use of the dispute resolution service;

(g) that the tenant considers that they are entitled to be paid the amount claimed; and

(h) that the tenant makes the statutory declaration knowing that if they knowingly and wilfully makes a false declaration they may be liable to prosecution under the Perjury Act 1911.

(Paragraph 4B(6) of schedule 10)

How does the TDS deal with applications?

Paragraph 4C of schedule 10 of HA 2004 sets out how the TDS is to deal with such applications.

When either the landlord or the tenant has made an application to the TDS, the scheme administrator must:

1. Serve notice together with a copy of the application and statutory declaration on the other party. The notice must do the following:

   (a) Ask the other party to indicate—

      (i) whether they accept that the applicant should be paid the whole or part of the deposit claimed;

      (ii) if they accept that part of the amount claimed should be paid, the amount they accept should be paid; and

      (iii) if they do not accept that the applicant should be paid the amount of the deposit claimed, whether they consent to the dispute being resolved through the use of the dispute resolution service.

   (b) Warn the other party that—

      (i) the amount claimed will be paid to the applicant unless, within the relevant period, the other party informs the scheme administrator that they do not accept that the whole of the amount claimed should be paid to the applicant; and

      (ii) if the other party responds to the scheme administrator informing him that they do not accept that the whole of the amount claimed should be paid to the applicant, but fail to respond within the relevant period to the question mentioned in paragraph (a)(iii), they will be treated as having given their consent for the dispute to be resolved through the use of the dispute resolution service.

The relevant period is 14 days beginning with the day the notice was received by the landlord or tenant. Sending the notice is also subject to the application meeting the requirements of paragraph 4A (7) and 4B (6) of schedule 10 as set out above.

If no response to the application is received within the relevant period, the money will be paid to the applicant as per the warning in the notice sent pursuant to paragraph 4C (2)(b) of schedule 10.

If within the relevant period, the scheme administrator receives notification from the receiving party that the claim is accepted, they can then proceed to grant the application and pay out the sums due within 10 days beginning on when the scheme administrator received the notification.

If within the relevant period, the scheme administrator receives notification from the receiving party that the Claim is not accepted, they must refuse the application and inform the applying party. If the opposing party states that they consent to the dispute being dealt with through the use of ADR (in accordance with 1 (a) (iii) above), the scheme administrator can then refer the matter to ADR.

If within the relevant period, the scheme administrator receives notification that part of the applicant's claim is accepted but part is not, they can pay out the accepted part and if the opposing party has stated they consent to the dispute being dealt with through ADR refer the dispute over the remaining sum to ADR.

If the opposing party fails to respond to whether they consent to ADR, it is deemed that they have given consent. The scheme administrator will inform the opposing party that deemed consent has been given and the dispute will proceed with ADR.

There is no provision set out within paragraph 4C of schedule 10 on what happens if all or part of the applicant's claim is disputed, and the opposing party has stated they do not give consent to ADR. It is presumed in this case that it is for the claiming party to issue court proceedings and obtain an order for the sums claimed. Upon receipt of that order the scheme administrator will then have to pay the sums due within 10 days of notification of the order.

Suitability and funding of the Custodial TDS

Custodial schemes are possibly more suitable for landlords who only have a small number of rental properties. One thing that has arisen is what happens if interest rates are low for a substantial time so that the accrued interest is not sufficient to fund the administration of the scheme. In that scenario the Government does have the power to offer additional funding under Chapter 4 of the HA 2004. It is suggested that the appropriate National Authority (presumably the Ministry of Housing, Communities and Local Government ('MHCLG') or body appointed by the MHCLG) may choose to give financial assistance to a TDS or provide a financial guarantee for a TDS if there is a danger of a TDS becoming insolvent (Section 212(4) and (5) of the HA 2004). There is no guarantee this will be granted though and the intention is that a TDS should be self-funded.

Insurance TDS

In an insurance TDS the landlord retains the deposit but pays a fixed premium to the scheme administrator. The fixed premium is in respect of the TDS's administration fees and the insurance premiums that are payable to protect the landlord's deposit in case of the landlord failing to return the full or part of the deposit to the tenant in cases where it should do so.

If the landlord wrongly withholds or misappropriates the deposit, the scheme administrator will pay the tenant the amount owed and will then endeavour to recover that sum from the landlord.

An insurance TDS must do the following:

1. Make provision as to the requirements that fall to be complied with by the landlord or by the scheme administrator where—

    (a) a landlord wishes to retain a deposit under the TDS or

    (b) a landlord retaining a deposit under the scheme (in relation to a AST that has not terminated) gives notice to the scheme administrator that they no longer wish to retain the deposit under that TDS

2. Provide that any landlord by whom a tenancy deposit is retained under the TDS must give the scheme administrator an undertaking to pay the deposit as directed.

3. Require the scheme administrator to effect, and maintain in force, adequate insurance in respect of failures by landlords to pay the deposit as required.

4. Provide details of what should happen if the landlord wishes to keep or release the deposit held under the TDS.

    (Paragraph 5 of schedule 10)

If there is a dispute between the landlord and tenant as to what proportion of the deposit should be repaid to the deposit, the tenant has to notify the scheme administrator that:

(a) the tenant has requested the landlord to repay to them the whole or any part of the deposit, and

(b) the amount in question ("the outstanding amount") has not been repaid to them within the period of 10 days beginning with the date on which the request was made.

The tenant must also indicate in their application whether they consent to the dispute being dealt with through ADR.

(Paragraph 6 (2) and (2A) of schedule 10)

On receiving the notification from the tenant, the scheme administrator must :

1. direct the landlord to pay an amount equal to the outstanding amount into a designated account held by the scheme administrator within 10 days beginning with the date the landlord receives this direction (paragraph 6 (3) of schedule 10)

2. send to the landlord a notice—

    (a) asking the landlord to indicate—

        (i) whether they accept that the tenant should be repaid the whole or part of the outstanding amount;

        (ii) if they accept that part of it should be repaid, the amount they accept should be repaid; and

(iii) if they do not accept that the tenant should be repaid the whole of the outstanding amount, whether they consent to the dispute being resolved through the use of the dispute resolution service; and

(b) warning the landlord that if they do not accept that the tenant should be repaid the whole of the outstanding amount but fail to respond within the relevant period to the question mentioned in paragraph (a)(iii) above, they will be treated as having given their consent for the dispute to be resolved through the use of that service (paragraph 6A (4) of schedule 10)

If within the relevant period, the scheme administrator does not receive a response from the landlord then:

(a) the scheme administrator must treat the lack of a response as an indication that the landlord does not accept that the tenant should be repaid any of the outstanding amount;

(b) the scheme administrator must determine forthwith whether they are satisfied that the notice was received by the landlord;

(c) if the scheme administrator determines that they are satisfied that it was so received, the landlord is to be treated as having given their consent for the dispute to be resolved through the use of the dispute resolution service; and

(d) the scheme administrator must inform the tenant and the landlord whether or not such consent is to be treated as having been given.

(Paragraph 6A (3) of schedule 10)

If within the relevant period, the scheme administrator receives notification from the receiving party that the claim is not accepted but fails to state if they are agreeable to the dispute being referred through ADR the landlord is deemed to have consented to the dispute being dealt with through ADR. The scheme administrator must inform the tenant and the landlord that consent is being treated as given (paragraph 6A (4) of schedule 10). The dispute would then be referred to ADR as it would if the landlord had consented.

Although not specified at paragraph 6A it is assumed as with the custodial scheme that if within the relevant period, the scheme administrator receives a response from the landlord that the claim is accepted, they will direct the landlord to make payment of the sums due. If the landlord has paid the sum to the scheme administrator, the scheme administrator will release the sums due within 10 days beginning on the date of the response.

If within the relevant period, the scheme administrator receives notification that part of the applicants claim is accepted but part is not, they will direct the landlord to pay out the agreed part and pay the remainder into a designated account until the dispute is resolved or if the sums due have already been paid by the landlord to the scheme administrator, the scheme administrator would pay out the agreed amount and hold the remainder until the dispute is resolved. This would fit in with paragraph 6 (3) to 6 (8) of schedule 10.

The relevant period is the period of 10 working days beginning with the day after the day on which the notice on the landlord under paragraph 6A (2) of schedule 10 is sent.

If the landlord and tenant come to an agreement on the outstanding sum or an arbitrator or Court determine that the whole or part of the deposit is payable to the tenant, the scheme administrator must then pay the tenant the amount due to him in accordance with that agreement, decision or Order within 10 days of the notification of the agreement, decision or order. If possible, this will be paid out of the money that the landlord has sent in accordance with paragraph 6 (3) of schedule 10. If the amount due is more than what has been obtained from the landlord, the scheme administrator will direct the landlord to pay the balance within 10 days of the scheme administrator's direction. If the amount due to the tenant is less than the money obtained from the landlord, the scheme administrator will pay the balance back to the landlord (paragraph 6 (3) to (8) of schedule 10)

If the landlord fails to pay the sums disputed to the scheme administrator, the scheme administrator will be expected to pay the sums due to the tenant and then pursue the landlord for the sums paid. This has raised concerns that the insurance TDS is vulnerable to insolvency if the landlord has not got the funds to pay the sums due to the tenant on the termination of the tenancy. A scheme administrator is therefore likely to check the status of the landlord before accepting them on a insurance TDS. You would, however, expect the insurance taken out to cover this scenario. In addition, as with a custodial TDS, the Government does have power to offer additional funding under Chapter 4 of the HA 2004 if there is a danger of a TDS becoming insolvent (Section 212(4) and (5) of the HA 2004).

Suitability of the Insurance TDS

Using an insurance TDS may be better suited to landlords with a large portfolio of properties and letting agents as they place a greater administrative burden on the landlord.

Dispute Resolution Procedures

As set out in the definition of a TDS at section 212 (2) of the HA 2004 a TDS should facilitate the resolution of deposit disputes without the need for referral through the Courts. Paragraph 10 of schedule 10 further states that each TDS must provide facilities to be available for enabling disputes relating to tenancy deposits subject to the scheme to be resolved without recourse to litigation. The referral through this scheme is, however, not compulsory and the tenant and/or landlord do not have to agree to it.

The MHCLG have indicated that the dispute resolution service would be provided free of charge.

Individual scheme administrators will have published guides to assist parties when confronted by a deposit dispute. The guides suggest how disputes can be avoided and the kind of evidence that an adjudicator will be expecting to see when dealing with a dispute. .

Court Proceedings

As set out above the landlord and tenant have recourse to enable disputes through the procedures offered by the TDS. However, both the landlord and the tenant retain the right to go to court. The dispute resolution procedure is a lot more cost effective for the parties as there is no fee. Issuing Court proceedings will attract a fee and legal costs if a solicitor is instructed. In addition, it is a dispute over the value of the deposit which is likely to be a fairly minimal amount especially since the TFA 2019 has placed a cap on the amount which can be taken at 5 weeks rent for those properties of a rental of less than £50,000.00 per annum or 6 weeks rent for those properties with a rental of £50,000.00 or more per annum. The costs of proceedings will outweigh that claimed and costs will not usually be recovered as it will be a small claims matter in the majority of cases unless it is an extremely high value property.

Summary

The objectives of a TDS are to ensure that deposits are protected and then returned to either the tenant in cases where the landlord has no claim over the sums due or to the landlord in whole or part when there is a legitimate claim and to resolve any disputes through dispute resolution where possible.

The landlord has a choice of a custodial or an insurance TDS. Both have the same objectives and which type of scheme is best suited for a particular landlord is likely to depend on their circumstances. A landlord should be fully aware of how each scheme works in order to make an informed decision and tenants should be aware of the procedures of the chosen scheme.

CHAPTER FOUR

INITIAL REQUIREMENTS AND PROVISION OF PRESCRIBED INFORMATION

Introduction

Under the HA 2004 (as amended) landlords have to Comply with the initial requirements of the TDS and serve prescribed information on the tenant within 30 days of receipt of a deposit. This chapter discusses the initial requirements and service of the prescribed information to aid and ensure compliance with the HA 2004.

Initial Requirements

Initial requirements are those requirements imposed by the particular TDS which the landlord is using (213(4) of the HA 2004). When registering the deposit, the landlord therefore needs to be particularly careful that they review the initial requirements and comply with the same within 30 days of receipt of the deposit. The initial requirements will not be exactly the same for each TDS scheme so if a landlord starts off with one TDS and then moves to another, they need to review the initial requirements of that new scheme to ensure they comply.

Prescribed Information

Prescribed information must be served on the tenant within 30 days of receipt of the deposit. Section 184 of the LA 2011 extended the period for compliance from 14 days. It should be noted that the extended period only applies where the deposit was received by the landlord on or after 6 April 2012 when section 184 of the LA 2011 came into force.

The prescribed information to be served is set out in The Housing (Tenancy Deposits) (Prescribed Information) Order 2007 ('the HTD Order') and is as follows:

(a) the name, address, telephone number, e-mail address and any fax number of the scheme administrator of the authorised TDS applying ;

(b) any information contained in a leaflet supplied by the scheme administrator to the landlord which explains the operation of the provisions contained in sections 212 to 215 of, and schedule 10 of the HA 2004;

(c) the procedures that apply under the TDS by which an amount in respect of a deposit may be paid or repaid to the tenant at the end of the AST;

(d) the procedures that apply under the TDS where either the landlord or the tenant is not contactable at the end of the AST;

(e) the procedures that apply under the TDS where the landlord and the tenant dispute the amount to be paid or repaid to the tenant in respect of the deposit;

(f) the facilities available under the scheme for enabling a dispute relating to the deposit to be resolved without recourse to litigation; and

(g) the following information in connection with the AST in respect of which the deposit has been paid—

   (i) the amount of the deposit paid;

(ii) the address of the property to which the tenancy relates;

(iii) the name, address, telephone number, and any e-mail address or fax

(iv) number of the landlord;

(v) the name, address, telephone number, and any e-mail address or fax number of the tenant, including such details that should be used by the landlord or scheme administrator for the purpose of contacting the tenant at the end of the AST;

(vi) the name, address, telephone number and any e-mail address or fax number of any relevant person;

(vii) the circumstances when all or part of the deposit may be retained by the landlord, by reference to the terms of the AST; and

(viii) confirmation (in the form of a certificate signed by the landlord) that—

(aa) the information he provides under this sub-paragraph is accurate to the best of his knowledge and belief; and

(bb) he has given the tenant the opportunity to sign any document containing the information provided by the landlord under this article by way of confirmation that the information is accurate to the best of his knowledge and belief.

As stated at 9 (vii) the landlord must certify the prescribed information to state that the information they have provided is correct and that they have given the tenant the opportunity of confirming that the information is correct.

The prescribed information must be served on:

1. the tenant; and;

2. any relevant person – a relevant person is someone who pays the deposit on behalf of the tenant in accordance with the tenancy arrangements (section 213(10) HA 2004).

The deposit must be protected no matter by whom it has been paid and a landlord must serve a copy of the prescribed information on any third party that has paid the deposit to the landlord on behalf of the tenant.

Initially it was only the landlord that could serve the prescribed information. Section 30 of the DA 2015 amended the HTD Order with effect from 26 March 2015 so that a person acting on the landlord's behalf could comply and serve the prescribed information. The landlord's agent is also able to provide their details rather than the landlord and certify the prescribed information. This was a relief to many landlords as it means they can effectively pass on the responsibility to their agent. The landlord should still however, check that their agent has complied.

A common misconception by landlords is that the TDS will serve the prescribed information and that they do not need to do so. It is true that under a custodial scheme information will be provided to the landlord and the tenant on receipt of the deposit. However, the landlord needs to check what has been served and what has been received. It is unlikely it will include the relevant terms of the tenancy agreement regarding possible reasons for withholding the deposit. A landlord would be well advised to serve the prescribed information themselves and certainly should not rely on the assumption that the TDS has served the prescribed information without checking exactly what has been served, whether this covers all the information required under the HTD Order and that there is confirmation of delivery on the tenant and any other relevant person.

The prescribed information also needs to be served in respect of every new AST. If a new fixed term AST has been granted to the same tenant for the same property or a statutory periodic tenancy has arisen at the end of the fixed term, this is not necessary as long as the deposit had already been protected, the prescribed information served at the outset of the original AST and the same DPS is being used. If there has been any change in the tenant, the property or the DPS scheme the prescribed information needs to be re-served within 30 days of the new AST being granted.

Relevant Case Law

Suurpere v Nice and another [2011]

On 6 January 2009, the landlords, Mr and Mrs Nice let a property by way of an AST to Ms Suurpere. Mr and Mrs Nice took a deposit of £500.00 at the outset of the AST but did not register the deposit in a DPS until 20 July 2009. On 21 July 2009, the DPS provided some information to Ms Suurpere regarding her deposit. The DPS provided a repayment ID and details of how to download a copy of the scheme and contact details. On 10 August 2009, Ms Suurpere issued proceedings against Mr and Mrs Nice for their failure to register the deposit within the time limits prescribed and their failure to serve the prescribed information. Ms Suurpere claimed she was entitled to 3 times the deposit in compensation due to the breach. On 14 August 2009, Ms Suurpere left the property and on 1 September Mr and Mrs Nice returned the deposit. In the first instance, Ms Suurpere's claim was dismissed as the deposit had been registered in a DPS before she had issued proceedings. Ms Suurpere appealed and on appeal it was held that Mr and Mrs Nice were in breach of s213(5) and (6)(a) of the HA 2004 as they had not served the prescribed information as required. Only part of the prescribed information required had been supplied by the DPS and they should not have relied on the DPS to serve Ms Suurpere. Ms Suurpere was entitled to compensation for the breach of the legislation.

Ayannuga v Swindells [2012]

The landlord let a property to the tenant under an AST for a term of 12 months at a monthly rent of £950.00. At the outset of the tenancy the landlord took a deposit of £950.00. The deposit was registered in a custodial TDS, but the landlord did not serve the prescribed information. The tenant fell into rent arrears and the landlord issued proceedings for possession of the property. In response the tenant claimed compensation for failure to serve the prescribed information. The landlord argued that the information had been provided in the AST and in a letter to the tenant. On the day of the hearing the landlord gave the tenant a document containing the additional information required. In the first instance, the Judge held that the landlord had satisfied his requirement through the information in the AST and the information provided before the judgment. The landlord was therefore not in breach and did not have to pay compensation. The tenant appealed and was successful. The landlord was clearly in breach of the legislation and had not complied with section 214 of the HA 2004. The requirement to serve prescribed information should not be treated as merely procedural as it informs the tenant of important information regarding how they can seek the recovery of their money and deal with disputes. The tenant should not have to carry out their own investigations and it is irrelevant if the information is freely available on the website for the TDS. The tenant was awarded compensation of 3 times the deposit.

Northwood (Solihull) Ltd v Fearn & Ors [2022]

The tenant argued that where the landlord or agent is a company the section 8 notice and prescribed information should be signed by a director and a witness, by 2 directors or by affixing the companies common seal to the document in accordance with section 44 of the Companies Act 2006. The landlord argued that an employee of a company can sign just as an agent can sign for a landlord. In the first instance the landlord was found to be in breach of the HTD Order. The landlord appealed and was successful. It was found that a signature by a director of the company that was authorised by the landlord was sufficient.

Summary

Landlords need to be careful that they comply with the initial requirements of the TDS and serve the prescribed information on the tenant within 30 days of receipt of the deposit. Care needs to be taken to serve all the prescribed information set out in the TFD Order and include the information relevant to the particular tenancy. Landlords should not rely on the TDS to serve the prescribed information as some of the information required is likely to be omitted. An omission of any of the required prescribed information could lead to sanctions and monetary claims against the landlord.

CHAPTER FIVE

SANCTIONS FOR NON-COMPLIANCE AND FINANCIAL PENALTIES

Introduction

If a landlord fails to comply with the legislation, it follows that there are going to be sanctions for non-compliance. This chapter aims to summarise those sanctions and financial penalties that may be applicable.

Prohibition from serving a section 21 notice

To regain possession of a property let under an AST the landlord currently has two routes. The first being under section 8 of the HA 1988 and the second under section 21 of the HA 1988. A detailed analysis of these routes is beyond the scope of this book.

The section 21 route allows the landlord to terminate an AST on or after the end of the fixed term by giving 2 months' notice. There does not have to be fault grounds or any reason for service of the Section 21 notice and a possession order is mandatory as long as the landlord has complied with the requirements of the DA 2015.

The section 8 route can be on any of the grounds set out at schedule 2 of the HA 1988. These grounds are a mixture of fault and non-fault grounds. The non-fault grounds are fairly restrictive, and a landlord will usually use the section 8 route for fault grounds such as rent arrears or anti-social behaviour. It tends to be a longer process and a number of the grounds in schedule 2 of the HA 1988 are discretionary, so a possession order is not guaranteed at the end of the process. For this reason, the section 21 route tends to be the preferred route.

Under section 215 of the HA 2004, a landlord cannot serve a valid section 21 notice if:

1. The landlord has not registered the deposit in a TDS, or the initial requirements of the TDS have not been complied with (section 215(1) of HA 2004) ; or;

2. The landlord has not served the prescribed information (section 215 (2) HA 2004).

3. If the deposit given comprised property rather than money in breach of section 213 (7) of the HA 2004.

The landlord has not registered the deposit in a TDS, or has not complied with the initial requirements of the TDS

The landlord is prohibited from serving a section 21 notice if they have received a deposit under the AST and failed to register the deposit with a TDS or failed to comply with the initial requirements of a TDS. The landlord can however rectify the situation by either:

(a) Returning the deposit to the tenant;

(b) Following determination, settlement, or withdrawal of any claim under section 214 (1) of the HA 2004.

Once the deposit has been returned the landlord can serve a section 21 notice.

The landlord cannot rectify the situation by simply registering the deposit with a TDS. The same applies if the landlord has registered the deposit late. In those circumstances, the landlord must also return the deposit if they want to serve a valid section 21 notice.

It is also important to note that even after the deposit is returned there is still a potential monetary claim for compensation. This is discussed below under financial penalties.

The landlord has not served the prescribed information

The landlord is prohibited from serving a valid section 21 notice if they have not served the prescribed information. The landlord can rectify this situation by returning the deposit or by serving the prescribed information. Once the prescribed information has been served, the landlord can proceed with serving a section 21 notice.

Again, even if the landlord returns the deposit or serves the prescribed information, they could still be subject to a claim by the tenant for monetary compensation.

The deposit given comprised property rather than money in breach of section 213 (7) of the HA 2004

The landlord is prohibited from serving a valid section 21 notice if the deposit given comprised property rather than money in breach of section 213 (7) of the HA 2004. The landlord can rectify this situation by returning the deposit to the person who provided it (section 215 (3) of the HA 2004)

Section 8 Notice

If the landlord does not rectify the issues in the way set out above, the landlord cannot serve a section 21 notice. The landlord can still serve a section 8 notice. However, there is a risk that the tenant will issue a counterclaim in response in respect of monetary compensation. This is likely to be more of a concern in respect of obtaining possession if a section 8 notice has been issued on rent arrears as if the compensation claim is larger than the arrears due there may not be sufficient arrears to warrant a mandatory order for possession.

Financial Penalties

A tenant can make a claim to the Court if:-

(a) The landlord has not registered the deposit (section 214 (1)(a) of the HA 2004);

(b) The landlord has not complied the initial requirements of the TDS or served the prescribed information (section 214 (1)(a) of the HA 2004);

(c) The landlord has been late registering the deposit, complying with the initial requirements and/or serving the prescribed information (section 214 (1)(a) of the HA 2004);

(d) They have been notified by the landlord that a TDS applies to the deposit paid but they have been unable to get confirmation from the scheme administrator that the deposit is held in accordance with that TDS (section 214(1)(b) of the HA 2004).

A tenant can make a claim to the Court whether the AST is continuing or at an end (section 214(1A) of the HA 2004). Section 214 (1A) was inserted by section 184 of LA 2011. Prior to the insertion, a tenant could not make a claim for financial penalties when the AST was at an end.

How a Court deals with an application does however depend on if the AST is continuing or if it's at an end.

If the tenancy is continuing the Court must either:-

(a) order the landlord to return the deposit to the tenant within 14 days (section 214 (3)(a) of the HA 2004) or;

(b) order the landlord pays a deposit into a designated account held by a scheme administrator and an authorised custodial TDS (section 214 (3) b) of the HA 2004)

If the tenancy has ended the Court may order the landlord to return all or part of the deposit to the tenant within 14 days.

If the tenancy has ended there is therefore a chance that the landlord may not be ordered to repay the deposit. However, it is the likely outcome.

In all cases, the Court must also order the landlord to pay compensation to the tenant at the value of 1 to 3 times the amount of the deposit. This has to be paid within 14 days of any order (section 214 (4)) of the Housing Act 2004).

The amount of compensation

As set out above, the Court must award 1 to 3 times the amount of the deposit as compensation if the landlord has not complied with the legislation. The question is how the Court will decide if they should award 1, 2 or 3 times the deposit to the tenant. This will largely depend on the facts of the particular case and whether the landlord has flagrantly disregarded the rules or made a genuine error. It will also depend on the gravity of the error. A Court is likely to look at a landlord who has registered the deposit a couple of days late more favourably than a landlord who has not registered the deposit at all.

By way of guidance, it is only likely to be 1 times the deposit if there has been a very minor fault such as serving the prescribed information a couple of days late. It is likely to be 2 times the deposit if it is believed that the landlord ought to have known that they should have registered the deposit and serve the prescribed information but failed to do so and 3 times the deposit if there has been a flagrant disregard of the legislation. It is likely an experienced landlord with a large portfolio of properties who is fully aware of the legislation will be penalised more than a landlord who has one property and has made an error as they were not aware or did not understand the legislation.

In most scenarios, it is expected that 2 times the deposit will be awarded as 3 times the deposit seems to involve some dishonesty and a continual failure to comply, and a fault would have to be very minor to warrant only 1 times the deposit.

Relevant cases

Qkadigbo & Anor v Chan [2014]

The property was let under an AST that commenced on 1 August 2012. The tenant paid a deposit at the outset. The landlord did not register the deposit in a TDS until 5 March 2013 and did not serve the prescribed information until 8 July 2013. The landlord was not experienced, and it was the first property that they had let out. The landlord had also employed managing agents to look after the property who had effectively let the landlord down by complying late. It was found that although the landlord was in breach it was the lowest level of noncompliance, and the compensation was limited to 1 times the deposit.

Khuja v Choudhury [2015]

On 7 July 2011 the landlord, let a property under an AST. The tenant paid a deposit of £800.00 in June 2011 in respect of the AST. The landlord did not register the deposit in a TDS until June 2013 and then re-registered the deposit in February 2014. The landlord did not serve the prescribed information. In 2014, the landlord served a notice pursuant to section 21 of the HA 1988 which was held to be invalid as the landlord had not served the prescribed information. The landlord then served the prescribed information and served a further section 21 notice. The tenant defended the possession proceedings on the basis that the prescribed information had ben served after the 30-day limit and the deposit had not been returned. At the same time, the tenant issued a counterclaim for compensation for breach of the legislation. It was found that as the deposit had been registered outside of the 30 days and the deposit had not been returned, the landlord could still not obtain possession under section 21. The Judge then dealt with the return of the deposit and the compensation payable for the breach. Firstly, it was ordered that the deposit be returned to the tenant. As set out above, the Judge has to order that the deposit is returned or paid into a TDS. The judge could therefore not order the landlord to leave the deposit registered. In respect of compensation, the Judge said he needed to take into consideration the conduct of the landlord. The landlord was a professional landlord that should have been aware of the legislation and should have had the systems in place to comply with the legislation when the deposit was received. However, even though the landlord 'ought to have known' it was not believed that the landlord has been dishonest or flagrantly disregarded the rules. The landlord had registered the deposit and served the prescribed information eventually. Taking into consideration the circumstances, the Judge awarded 2 times the deposit which equated to £1,600.00.

Sanctions applicable to an insurance TDS

The scheme administrator under an insurance TDS can also:

(a) Require the landlord to pay the deposit as they direct.

(b) Direct that the deposit will no longer be held under the insurance TDS.
(c) Direct that the landlord can no longer be a member of the insurance TDS.
(d) Pay the tenant the deposit that is properly due to be returned to the tenant and pursue the landlord for the remainder.

The terms of an Insurance TDS ae discussed at more detail in chapter 3 above.

Liability of Agents

If an agent receives the deposit and fails to register it, they can be held liable and be subject to proceedings for the monetary compensation due for the breach i.e., 1 to 3 times the deposit paid. The tenant can bring proceedings directly against the agent. They do not have to be through the landlord.

Relevant Case

Draycott & another v Hannells Letting Ltd [2010]

On 28 February 2008, the tenants entered into a 12-month AST with Derby Build Limited, the landlord. On 4 March 2008, the tenants paid a deposit of £2,700.00 to Hannells Lettings Ltd ('Hannells'), who were the landlord's agent. There was an obligation in the AST for the tenant to pay the deposit to Hannells not the landlord. On 19 May 2008 Hannells registered the deposit into a TDS and on 21 May 2008 they served the prescribed information on the tenants. On 27 November 2008, the tenants issued proceedings against Hannells for failing to register the deposit and serve the prescribed information within the 14 days required.

One of the arguments raised by Hannells was that a claim for compensation under section 214 of HA 2004 could only be issued against the landlord.

It was held that section 212 (9) of the HA 2004 defines 'landlord' to include a person acting on the landlord's behalf and that this should apply to a claim under section 214 of the HA 2004. Further, section 214 (3)(a) of HA 2004 states that the sanctions for non-compliance are to be imposed against the person who it appears to the Court is holding the deposit. As Hannells had taken the deposit on behalf of the landlord and was continuing to hold the deposit they could be held liable, and proceedings could be issued against them. However, in this case, Hannells were not held liable as it was determined that it was not an initial requirement of the custodial DPS that they pay the deposit into the DPS within 14 days and that as long as they paid it before the tenant commenced proceedings, they were not liable.

Multiple Tenants

If there is more than one tenant any application for a return of the deposit and compensation should be made by all of the tenants jointly *(Gladehurst Properties Limited v Hashemi [2011]).*

Limitation for issuing a claim for compensation

There is no guidance on how long a tenant has to issue a claim under section 214 of the HA 2004. It is assumed that limitation will follow that provided for in the Limitation Act 1980 which states that the standard time limit for contractual claims is six years starting from the date that a cause of action' arises.

The question is whether the clock starts running from the expiry of the time limit for the landlord to register the deposit and/or file the prescribed information or from the end of the AST as that is when the deposit becomes repayable.

It may be seen as unfair to the tenants if limitation runs from the date of the landlord's non-compliance as the tenant may not be aware of the breach until the AST ends and they seek a refund of the deposit. A tenant may also not want to issue a claim whilst they remain in occupation for fear of a retaliatory eviction.

The question of the correct limitation period does not appear to have been tested in the Courts and it may depend on the circumstances of the case as to when time starts ticking for the purposes of limitation.

Summary

If a landlord fails to comply with the legislation, they will not be able to serve a valid section 21 notice until they have rectified the error and will also be liable to pay compensation up to 3 times the value of the deposit. Agents may also be liable to pay compensation if they are holding the deposit.

CHAPTER SIX

THE POSITION OF DEPOSITS IN PERIODIC/RENEWAL TENANCIES

Introduction

The legislation on deposits, the various amendments of the same and recent case law has led to much confusion about when the deposit requirements apply in different scenarios such as when deposits have been taken prior to the introduction of the legislation but a renewal tenancy has been granted. This chapter aims to address and clarify the position in respect of some possible scenarios.

The legal position of ASTs when the fixed term expires

At the end of the fixed term AST a new AST is formed which is either a new fixed tenancy or a periodic tenancy. As it is a new AST, the initial deposit taken is deemed as a fresh deposit. The question that then arises is, in what circumstances should this fresh deposit be registered/re-registered and/or the prescribed information served/re-served. This is discussed in the context of various scenarios below.

Relevant Case

Superstrike Limited -v- Rodrigues [2013]

The landlord let the property to the tenant under a fixed term AST in January 2007. A deposit was taken at the outset of the AST. The deposit was not registered as it was taken prior to the introduction of the legislation on 6 April 2007. The fixed term AST ended in January 2008. The tenant remained in occupation under a statutory periodic tenancy. The landlord commenced proceedings under section 21 of the HA 1988. The tenant defended the proceedings stating that the landlord was unable to use the section 21 procedure as the deposit had not been registered when the tenancy became a statutory periodic tenancy in January 2008. It was held that a new tenancy was formed in January 2008, a new deposit was deemed to have been received and the landlord should have registered the deposit in accordance with the legislation that is now in place. By failing to do so, the landlord could not rely on section 21 of the HA 1988 to obtain possession.

Scenario 1 – Deposit for the original tenancy received before 6th April 2007 and a statutory periodic tenancy arose before 6th April 2007

Should the deposit be registered?

In this situation, there is no obligation to register the deposit.

Can the landlord serve a notice under section 21 of the HA 1988?

Despite the fact that there is no requirement for the landlord to register the deposit in this scenario the landlord cannot serve a notice under section 21 of the HA 1988 if they have failed to do so. To serve a section 21 notice, the landlord will firstly need to either register the deposit or return it to the tenant. It is therefore advised that landlords register the deposit as and when they can.

Relevant Case

Charalambous & another -v- Maureen Rosairieng and another [2014]

This case concerned this very scenario. On 20 August 2002, the tenants entered into a fixed term AST for the period of 12 months. The tenants paid a deposit at the outset. The parties agreed to a number of further fixed terms ASTs. The last fixed term AST granted expired on 17 August 2005. The tenants remained in occupation and a statutory periodic tenancy arose. The landlord retained the deposit taken in respect of the original tenancy on 20 August 2022 throughout.

In 2012 the landlord served a notice under section 21 of the HA 1988. The tenants stated it was invalid as the deposit has not been registered with a TDS. It was held that there was no obligation to register the deposit that was received prior to 6 April 2007 as there was no authorised scheme with which a landlord could have protected the deposit and the relevant provisions of the Housing Act 2004 were not in place at the time. However, it was still held that the prohibition on serving a notice under section 21 of the HA 1988 applied and that the deposit would need to registered in a TDS or returned to the tenants before serving a section 21 notice.

Section 31 of the DA 2015

The finding in the case of *Charalambous* was confirmed by the coming into force of Section 31 of the DA 2015 which states a landlord is not obliged to protect the deposit in a TDS in this scenario but that the landlord cannot serve a Section 21 notice unless the deposit is protected or repaid (Section 215(1) and 214).

There is still no financial penalty to the landlord in this situation (Section 214(1) DA 2015).

Scenario 2 – Deposit for the original tenancy received before 6th April 2007 and a statutory periodic tenancy has arisen on or after 6th April 2007 and the deposit is not protected

Should the deposit be registered?

In this situation the landlord should have registered the deposit as the legislation was in place when the tenancy became a statutory periodic tenancy. The statutory periodic tenancy is a new tenancy and the deposit treated as a fresh deposit that should be registered. The prescribed information should also be served.

Can the landlord serve a notice under section 21 of the HA 1988?

As the deposit should have been registered it follows that the landlord will not be able to serve a section 21 notice. To do so, the landlord will need to return the deposit to the tenant.

Guidance in support

The Law Society Guidance: Deregulation Act 2015: Tenancy Deposit Scheme and Landlord's Obligations

This guidance states that all deposits taken before 6 April 2007 must be registered when an AST becomes a periodic tenancy on or after 6th April 2007.

Section 32 of the DA 2015

Section 32 of the DA 2015 inserted a new section 215A into the HA 2004 confirming that landlords must protect deposits in this scenario and serve the prescribed information. In order to try and assist landlords section 215A allowed for a grace period of 90 days for compliance i.e., by 23 June 2015.

Scenario 3 – A renewal or statutory periodic tenancy arose on or after 6th April 2007 and a deposit was received and protected before 6th April 2007

Should the deposit be re-registered and prescribed information re-served?

It was thought by some that the finding in *Superstrike* meant that every time a new tenancy arose the landlord would need to protect the deposit again and re-serve prescribed information. However, in this situation as long as the deposit has already been protected and the prescribed information given, then if a renewal AST or a statutory periodic tenancy arises on or after 6th April 2007, there is no need to re-register the deposit or reserve prescribed information. This is on the proviso that there have been no changes in the identity of the tenant or the demise and the deposit remains protected in accordance with the same TDS.

Legislation in support

Section 215B of the HA 2004 (as amended by the DA 2015) deals with this very scenario and states that as long as the deposit remains protected in accordance with the authorised TDS from one AST to the next there is no requirement for the landlord to reregister or re-serve the same prescribed information to the tenant each time a renewal AST is granted or the AST rolls over into a periodic AST. This applies to not only the first renewal of the AST but also multiple tenancies which can include a mixture of fixed term and periodic tenancies. It also applies if the deposit received prior to 6th April 2007 is subsequently registered.

Transitional Provisions

Section 215C of the HA 2004 deals with the transitional provisions in relation to section 215A and 215B of the HA 2004. They are treated as having had effect since 6 April 2007. However, they do not have effect in relation to a claim under section 214 of the HA 2004 or section 21 of the HA 1988 that was settled or determined prior to 26 March 2015.

Summary

Care needs to be taken when a new AST is formed either by a renewal or periodic tenancy. Registering a deposit is advisable in all circumstances even if it was taken prior to the legislation coming into force as it will prohibit possession proceedings under section 21 if the landlord does not do so. If there is any change in the identity of the tenant/tenants, the demise or the TDS, landlords should discuss with the current TDS provider as to the steps to be taken and re-serve the prescribed information.

CHAPTER SEVEN

TENANCY DEPOSITS IN FLAT SHARES

Introduction

When deposits are taken in respect of flat shares the following issues may arise

1. Over time one or more tenants may move out and different tenants may move in.

2. The landlord may not be notified of these changes.

3. The tenants that remain may have reimbursed outgoing tenants with their share of the deposit so there will have been deposit changes as well as identity changes that the landlord is unaware of.

The aim of this chapter is to consider how the landlord should deal with these scenarios to ensure they comply with the deposit legislation.

Change of identity of the tenants

If one or more tenant moves out and different tenants move in there has been a change in the identity of tenant which will amount to a surrender of the original AST and the grant of a new AST. If the original tenancy was prior to 6 April 2007 and the deposit was not registered, the landlord should register the deposit on the grant of the new AST and serve prescribed information on the tenants. In addition, as there has been a change in identity of the tenants, even if the initial deposit was registered prior to the new AST, the deposit would need to be re-protected and new prescribed information served to match up with who the new tenants are.

Relevant Case

London Borough of Tower Hamlets -v- Iyinde [1994]

The tenant had moved out of the property and moved to Nigeria. The tenant informed the landlord that he and his family were moving out and that a cousin who already lived in the property would be taking over the tenancy. The landlord took no action in respect of this information and accepted rent from the cousin. It was held that by taking no action on receipt of the information, the landlord was deemed to have accepted the tenant's offer of a surrender. The change in identity of the tenant therefore amounted to a surrender of the original AST by operation of law and a grant of a new AST to the cousin. The deposit would need to be re-protected and the prescribed information reserved.

Landlord is not notified of changes in the identity of the tenants and/or deposit changes

In the case of *London Borough of Tower Hamlets v Iyinde* the landlord was informed that the identity of the tenant was changing but what happens if a landlord is not aware of any changes in the identity of the tenants occupying the flats. In addition, what is the position if there are changes in who has paid the deposit which the landlord is unaware of such as the remaining tenants refunding part of the deposit to an outgoing tenant and taking a further share of the deposit from a new incoming tenant.

It has been held that it doesn't matter if the tenant is unaware of the changes in the identity of the tenant or any deposit changes from the ingoing or outgoing tenants. It also doesn't matter if the deposit from the ingoing or outgoing tenants are paid directly to the landlord. The landlord will still be seen as having received the deposit from the tenants at each change of identity and expected to have known of the identity changes in most circumstances. The landlord needs to protect any deposits for as long as the flat share continues, and it doesn't matter if the AST started before the HA 2004 because each time there is an identity change a deposit needs to be registered because it is effectively a new tenancy.

This raises difficulties as to how the landlord deals with the deposit on each change of identity or how they ensure they are notified of each identity change and when new deposits etc are received. One possibility is to add clauses into the AST dealing with this eventuality and placing an obligation on the tenants to notify the landlord if they are moving out or of any change in the tenants in the property.

In respect of deposit and identity changes, once the deposit is registered it should be for the landlord to refund the appropriate part and re-protect the remainder and protect any additional deposit received from an incoming tenant. The landlord should re-protect the deposit on each change to ensure the details the TDS have match who the tenant or tenants actually are. Whilst doing this the TDS may allow the landlord to release the joint tenant's share. This is assuming the TDS used permits this. It is possible it does not. In addition, the portion the landlord is looking to refund may be in dispute in any event due to rent arrears or disrepair. In each case of a change, it is therefore suggested that the landlord discuss the change with their particular TDS to ensure compliance and that the deposit is re-protected and dealt with accordingly and the prescribed information served/re-served.

Under the terms of most custodial TDSs, the landlord can decide whether to register separate deposits in the names of each individual tenant when there are multiple tenants in occupation. Previously landlords have been minded to register the deposit in the name of a lead tenant. However, if the deposits are registered separately in properties of multiple occupation it would assist greatly in this scenario and will make it a lot easier to refund the deposit due to each tenant on their departure. Landlords should still check however, if the remaining tenant's deposits need to be re-protected and the prescribed information in each case should still be re-served as the details of who is in occupation would still have changed. This needs to be discussed with the TDS provider but it will be for landlords to ensure compliance.

Relevant Case

Sturgiss and Gupta -v- Boddy and Others [2021]

This case deals with this very scenario. Mr Boddy let out a flat in 2004 under an AST to 4 tenants. The rent under the AST was £349.00 per week which equates to £1,512.33 per month and the landlord held a deposit of £1,205.00. By May 2020, the rent due under the AST had increased to £2,295.00 per month. The method by which it had been increased is not specified in the case, but it was not disputed.

Miss Sturgiss moved into the property on 17 October 2018 and paid £1,050.00 to the outgoing tenants in respect of their deposit share and then paid £702.00 per month rent to Mr Boddy.

Miss Gupta moved into the property in April 2019 and paid the outgoing tenant £800.00 in respect of their deposit share and then paid £660.00 per month rent.

Miss Gupta decided she wanted to move out of the property in early 2020 and asked Mr Boddy whether the existing deposit was protected. Mr Boddy confirmed that the deposit was not protected as the initial deposit had been taken pre-6 April 2007 which was before there was any requirement to do so as the legislation was not in place.

Miss Gupta left in February 2020 as planned and a new incoming tenant paid Miss Gupta the £800.00 deposit she had paid when she had gone into the property.

In March 2020 Miss Sturgiss gave Mr Boddy notice that she would be moving out and would only be paying rent until 15 May 2020.

In August 2020, Miss Gupta and Miss Sturgiss issued proceedings against Mr Boddy for compensation under section 214 of the HA 2004 for failing to register the deposit. Miss Gupta and Miss Sturgiss argued that each time there had been a change in the tenants occupying the flat the existing AST had been surrendered and a new tenancy had arisen.

Mr Boddy argued in response that firstly that the occupiers were not tenants but were in fact licensees and secondly that the deposits taken from new incoming tenants were not paid to him in connection with any AST as they were paid to the remaining tenants on each occasion.

In the first instance, Mr Boddy was successful, and Miss Gupta and Miss Sturgiss' claim was dismissed. It was held that the occupiers were licensees without exclusive occupation as Mr Boddy had claimed and that each time a new occupier moved into the property there had not been a surrender and re-grant because Mr Boddy had played no part in the change. As it was a licence the deposit did not need to be registered.

In addition, the Court held that only the tenants who paid the original deposit would be able to issue a claim because they were the ones who had paid the deposit to Mr Boddy and who were entitled to a refund of the deposit.

Miss Gupta and Miss Sturgis appealed. On appeal the Court dealt with three issues. The first being whether it amounted to a tenancy or a licence, the second whether there was a surrender and re-grant if it was a tenancy each time there was an identity change and the third being how to deal with the deposit and whether it should have been registered and the penalty for failing to do so, if appropriate.

On the first issue the appeal was allowed. The Court said that it was a tenancy not a licence as it had all the hallmarks of a tenancy. There was exclusive possession, it was for a term, and the tenants were paying a rent.

On the second issue the Court again found for Miss Sturgiss and Miss Gupta. The Court said that every time a tenant left, and another entered it would amount to a surrender of the existing AST and a grant of a new AST. This is the case even if Mr Boddy did not know of the change. This coincided with the findings in the *London Borough of Tower Hamlets -v- Ayinde [1994].* Mr Boddy's evidence also made it clear that there had been a prior arrangement that the tenants wouldn't inform him if there was then a change in identity of the tenants as he didn't want to be involved.

As it had been found that there had been a surrender and re-grant, the third issue had to be dealt with as to whether the deposit should have been registered whenever a new periodic tenancy had been formed. Again, the appeal was allowed, and Miss Sturgiss and Miss Gupta were successful. On the creation of the first new AST the deposit should have been registered and prescribed information served on the current tenants. The deposit should have also been re- protected on each subsequent new AST granted as a result of the change in identity of the tenants and the prescribed information reserved.

As a consequence, Mr Boddy was liable to pay compensation up to three times the value of the deposit. In this case the original deposit was £1,205.00 and they felt that compensation for the breach should be that sum, and there shouldn't be any multiples applied to that sum for the following reasons:-

(a) The first deposit had been taken pre-6 April 2007 when there was no requirement to register the deposit;

(b) Mr Boddy had always retained the deposit and gave an undertaking to the Court that if it ruled against him, he would protect the deposit he had retained for over 15 years.

(c) Mr Boddy was not aware that the deposit should be registered. Firstly, because he believed it was a licence and secondly because the HA 2004 was not in place at the outset of the original tenancy.

(d) Mr Boddy didn't use a managing agent and had little or no visibility of the tenant's arrangements in the property.

(e) The situation in this scenario had not previously been clarified and it was not unreasonable for Mr Boddy to think the deposit did not need to be registered. His view had been supported by the Judge in the first instance and presumably by his legal advisors.

Even though the multiplier applied to the compensation was 1, Mr Boddy still had to pay the sum of £3,615.00 because there had been 3 occasions when Mr Boddy should have registered the deposit. Each time there had been a change in identity and a new AST had been formed, he had defaulted and was liable to pay compensation.

One thing to note is going forward a Court may not be as generous to landlords that fall foul of the same legislation as they were to Mr Boddy as there is now a case and landlords should now be fully aware of the position and not fail to register the deposit as and when it is necessary during the course of the flat share.

Summary

Extra care needs to be taken if you are a landlord letting a property to multiple tenants under a flat share. Precautions need to be taken to ensure the landlord is aware of any identity or deposit changes and that they re- protect the deposit and re-serve prescribed information on the current tenants at each identity and/or deposit change. Failure to do so could result in a financial penalty if either the current or past tenants issue proceedings.

CHAPTER EIGHT

SELLING A PROPERTY SUBJECT TO AN AST

Introduction

If you are buying a property that is subject to an AST, the buyer needs to ensure the deposit is protected and remains protected to avoid any breach of the legislation. There is nothing specific in the legislation on how to deal with a deposit on the sale of the property.

There was a number of discussions on this topic when the legislation was introduced and the MHCLG anticipated that the buyer and seller would sort out the deposit between themselves and take the relevant steps and that the tenant could assume that their deposit would remain protected.

This chapter summarises the steps the seller and the buyer may wish to and should take when purchasing the property to ensure compliance.

Sale Documentation

On a sale the buyer should check that the seller has properly protected the deposit. If it has failed to do so, this could cause serious problems for the buyer if it wishes to serve a section 21 notice to recover possession of the property.

The sale documentation should make provision in respect of the deposit. The buyer needs to know that the deposit is currently protected, and that the seller complied with the initial requirements and served the prescribed information within the 30 days limit. Ideally the sales documents should therefore contain confirmation from the buyer of the following;

- That the deposit has been registered with a TDS.
- Details of the TDS they have used and the contact details.
- That they protected the deposit withing 30 days of receiving the same.
- That they complied with the initial requirements of the TDS and served the prescribed the requisite information within 30 days or any time period required by the TDS.

Transfer of the Deposit

The TDS will need to be informed if there is a change in the landlord or agent dealing with the deposit. The terms of the TDS need to read carefully to make sure that the scheme has the facility to transfer deposit protection between landlords and that the terms will accommodate the circumstances anticipated.

Ideally, the seller should make the TDS aware that they are selling the property.

Each TDS has its own procedures for dealing with changes. The TDS will be able to inform the landlord of the procedures and must inform the parties if they stop protecting the deposit.

The new landlord or agent needs to make arrangements to ensure the deposit to remain protected and comply with the legislation and the guidance from the TDS. In some cases, the seller will insist the deposit is transferred/protected by the buyer between exchange and completion to ensure the deposit remains protected and there is no potential claim against them.

Once the seller transfers the protected deposit to the buyer, the buyer should re- serve the prescribed information on the tenant within 30 days of the transfer or within the time limit stated by the TDS, if less, as there has been a change in a material term of the tenancy under section 213 HA 2004.

What if the property is charged and the mortgagee goes into possession?

The principles set out above for when a property is sold will equally apply where a property is charged, and the mortgagee goes into possession.

What steps can tenants take to check their deposit remains registered?

A tenant can check whether their deposit is still protected with the TDS if there has been a change in the landlord. The tenant should have the details from receiving the prescribed information. If they have not received the prescribed information or any details of registration of their deposit, they can request the same from the old and/or the new landlord and if that fails, apply to the Court on the basis that there has breach by failing to serve the prescribed information. If the TDS confirms the deposit is no longer protected and/or has not been transferred into the new landlord's name, the tenant will again have a cause of action through the Courts for compensation.

In the discussions after the introduction of the legislation, the MHCLG did warn tenants that if their deposit was registered in an insurance TDS, the incoming landlord may not have been provided with the details by the outgoing landlord and the tenant may need to chase up the scheme administrator to make sure that everyone knows the position.

Summary

The starting position in dealing with selling a property subject to an AST is to contact the TDS and check the position. The seller will then be in a position to advise the buyer who is likely to require this information as part of their enquiries and/or the sales contract. Both parties then need to comply with what is required by the TDS and in all cases the buyer should re-serve the prescribed information once the deposit has been transferred into their name.

CHAPTER NINE

FORTHCOMING LEGISLATION

Introduction

This book has aimed to provide you with guidance on the current key legislation on tenancy deposits in ASTs and the factors to consider when assessing tenancy deposit disputes. Hopefully, the contents will assist as a starting point in any tenancy deposit queries which will be relevant to not only tenancy deposit disputes and monetary compensation claims by tenants but also in advising a landlord on section 21 possession proceedings.

In respect of the legislation there has been a proposed change in how tenancy deposits are dealt with in the pipeline for some time. In April 2019, the government announced proposals for a Renters Reform Bill. These proposals incorporate the introduction of lifetime deposits which I will discuss below.

Lifetime Deposits

The purpose of the introduction of lifetime deposits is to allow tenants to not have to pay a new deposit every time they move to a new house. There has been growing concern that tenants are not being to move to a new property when they wish to do so because they cannot raise the money for a new deposit. This results in tenants sometimes staying in a property in disrepair or not being able to re-locate when they wish to do so.

The lifetime deposit will allow a deposit paid by a tenant to be transferred from one landlord to another when a tenant moves with the tenant only needing to pay any top up, if required. This would hopefully prevent tenants from facing the restrictive cash flow they are currently experiencing.

The idea appears to be that tenants will hold a digital certificate with details of their deposit. When they move, the certificate will be presented, and the current landlord will be required to transfer the money to the new landlord.

There are a number of potential issues with the proposal as it stands, and the hope is that these issues will be ironed out before the Renters Reform Bill is introduced. Some of the issues are set out below.

How will lifetime deposits work in flat shares?

Chapter 7 deals with some of the concerns and issues that already arise in shared tenancies when the identity of the tenants change.

The case of *Sturgiss* suggests that each time a new tenant replaces another the law may on the basis of its decision at least treat the existing AST as surrendered and a new AST granted. The deposit will need to re-protected and the prescribed information re-served.

What will therefore happen with a lifetime deposit if one tenant moves out and needs their deposit (or share of) to be transferred but the other tenants are remaining in the property. Will there be top up provisions for the other tenant in the flat share? The logistics on how a lifetime deposit will work in this situation is not provided for in the current proposals or guidance on the forthcoming bill.

What if the tenant leaves the property in disrepair?

It is common, in my experience, for tenants to leave a property in disrepair when they vacate. The fact this is a common occurrence is one of the reasons landlords require a deposit. Usually, when a tenant leaves the property, the landlord will then attend the property to assess if there is any disrepair before contacting the TDS to deal with the return of the deposit to the tenant. If existing landlords have to transfer the deposit to a new landlord before the tenant moves, how will they get chance to assess the damage and receive part of the deposit for any damages incurred. It is likely the new landlord will want the deposit transferred before the tenant moves in.

It is vital that the introduction of lifetime deposits does not give up the right of landlords to make a claim for damages from the deposit. This is the very purpose of the deposit, and a landlord shouldn't have to give up their deposit before they're satisfied that there is no claim for all, or part of the deposit retained.

There has been some discussion on how to deal with this issue since the Renters Reform Bill was proposed and a couple of ideas have been considered as follows:

(a) A financial bridging facility – This would need to ensure the new landlord is covered by a full deposit even if the current deposit is in dispute or partly in dispute with the current landlord. It could possibly be a short-term interest free loan to the tenant.

(b) A deposit builder ISA – This would involve a government protected savings pot that is available to tenants. There would have to be a minimum fund of the value of the deposit at the outset of the original tenancy. Neither the landlord or tenant would be able to have access to the money deposited into the account unless it was ordered by the TDS and tenants would be able to save in the account beyond the minimum deposit required eventually using funds to relocate as an when required.

How will lifetime deposits work alongside the existing TDS?

A further consideration is how will lifetime deposits work alongside existing TDSs. How will the transfer of lifetime deposits between TDSs be smooth and how will it work if the current and new landlords use a different type of TDS, i.e. the current tenant could have a custodial TDS and the new landlord an insurance TDS. The custodial and insurance TDS are very different with different mechanisms and guidance is needed on how any transfer will take place.

Summary

There needs to be some clarification on how lifetime deposits will work. It is thought that if the above issues can be dealt with the introduction of lifetime deposits will be a benefit to letting agents and the letting market in general as it will remove the financial issues many tenants currently experience when they are trying to relocate. If there are cheaper moving costs, more tenants may be moving to new properties and there may ultimately be more renters. This will also be of a benefit to landlords and encourage more buy to let properties.

There is currently no date for the implementation of the Renters Reform Bill, but it seems certain that it will be implemented and that this will take place in the near future.

MORE BOOKS BY LAW BRIEF PUBLISHING

'A Practical Guide to Religion and Belief Discrimination Claims in the Workplace' by Kashif Ali
'A Practical Guide to the Law of Medical Treatment Decisions' by Ben Troke
'Fundamental Dishonesty and QOCS in Personal Injury Proceedings: Law and Practice' by Jake Rowley
'A Practical Guide to the Law in Relation to School Exclusions' by Charlotte Hadfield & Alice de Coverley
'A Practical Guide to Divorce for the Silver Separators' by Karin Walker
'The Right to be Forgotten – The Law and Practical Issues' by Melissa Stock
'A Practical Guide to Planning Law and Rights of Way in National Parks, the Broads and AONBs' by James Maurici QC, James Neill et al
'A Practical Guide to Election Law' by Tom Tabori
'A Practical Guide to the Law in Relation to Surrogacy' by Andrew Powell
'A Practical Guide to Claims Arising from Fatal Accidents – 2nd Edition' by James Patience
'A Practical Guide to the Ownership of Employee Inventions – From Entitlement to Compensation' by James Tumbridge & Ashley Roughton
'A Practical Guide to Asbestos Claims' by Jonathan Owen & Gareth McAloon
'A Practical Guide to Stamp Duty Land Tax in England and Northern Ireland' by Suzanne O'Hara
'A Practical Guide to the Law of Farming Partnerships' by Philip Whitcomb
'Covid-19, Homeworking and the Law – The Essential Guide to Employment and GDPR Issues' by Forbes Solicitors
'Covid-19 and Criminal Law – The Essential Guide' by Ramya Nagesh
'Covid-19 and Family Law in England and Wales – The Essential Guide' by Safda Mahmood
'A Practical Guide to the Law of Unlawful Eviction and Harassment – 2nd Edition' by Stephanie Lovegrove
'Covid-19, Brexit and the Law of Commercial Leases – The Essential Guide' by Mark Shelton
'A Practical Guide to Costs in Personal Injury Claims – 2nd Edition' by Matthew Hoe

'A Practical Guide to the General Data Protection Regulation (GDPR) – 2nd Edition' by Keith Markham
'Ellis on Credit Hire – Sixth Edition' by Aidan Ellis & Tim Kevan
'A Practical Guide to Working with Litigants in Person and McKenzie Friends in Family Cases' by Stuart Barlow
'Protecting Unregistered Brands: A Practical Guide to the Law of Passing Off' by Lorna Brazell
'A Practical Guide to Secondary Liability and Joint Enterprise Post-Jogee' by Joanne Cecil & James Mehigan
'A Practical Guide to the Pre-Action RTA Claims Protocol for Personal Injury Lawyers' by Antonia Ford
'A Practical Guide to Neighbour Disputes and the Law' by Alexander Walsh
'A Practical Guide to Forfeiture of Leases' by Mark Shelton
'A Practical Guide to Coercive Control for Legal Practitioners and Victims' by Rachel Horman
'A Practical Guide to Rights Over Airspace and Subsoil' by Daniel Gatty
'Tackling Disclosure in the Criminal Courts – A Practitioner's Guide' by Narita Bahra QC & Don Ramble
'A Practical Guide to the Law of Driverless Cars – Second Edition' by Alex Glassbrook, Emma Northey & Scarlett Milligan
'A Practical Guide to TOLATA Claims' by Greg Williams
'A Practical Guide to Elderly Law – 2nd Edition' by Justin Patten
'A Practical Guide to the Law of Prescription in Scotland' by Andrew Foyle
'A Practical Guide to the Construction and Rectification of Wills and Trust Instruments' by Edward Hewitt
'A Practical Guide to the Law of Bullying and Harassment in the Workplace' by Philip Hyland
'How to Be a Freelance Solicitor: A Practical Guide to the SRA-Regulated Freelance Solicitor Model' by Paul Bennett
'A Practical Guide to Prison Injury Claims' by Malcolm Johnson
'A Practical Guide to the Small Claims Track - 2nd Edition' by Dominic Bright
'A Practical Guide to Advising Clients at the Police Station' by Colin Stephen McKeown-Beaumont

'A Practical Guide to Antisocial Behaviour Injunctions' by Iain Wightwick
'Practical Mediation: A Guide for Mediators, Advocates, Advisers, Lawyers, and Students in Civil, Commercial, Business, Property, Workplace, and Employment Cases' by Jonathan Dingle with John Sephton
'The Mini-Pupillage Workbook' by David Boyle
'A Practical Guide to Crofting Law' by Brian Inkster
'A Practical Guide to Spousal Maintenance' by Liz Cowell
'A Practical Guide to the Law of Domain Names and Cybersquatting' by Andrew Clemson
'A Practical Guide to the Law of Gender Pay Gap Reporting' by Harini Iyengar
'A Practical Guide to the Rights of Grandparents in Children Proceedings' by Stuart Barlow
'NHS Whistleblowing and the Law' by Joseph England
'Employment Law and the Gig Economy' by Nigel Mackay & Annie Powell
'A Practical Guide to Noise Induced Hearing Loss (NIHL) Claims' by Andrew Mckie, Ian Skeate, Gareth McAloon
'An Introduction to Beauty Negligence Claims – A Practical Guide for the Personal Injury Practitioner' by Greg Almond
'Intercompany Agreements for Transfer Pricing Compliance' by Paul Sutton
'Zen and the Art of Mediation' by Martin Plowman
'A Practical Guide to the SRA Principles, Individual and Law Firm Codes of Conduct 2019 – What Every Law Firm Needs to Know' by Paul Bennett
'A Practical Guide to Adoption for Family Lawyers' by Graham Pegg
'A Practical Guide to Industrial Disease Claims' by Andrew Mckie & Ian Skeate
'A Practical Guide to Redundancy' by Philip Hyland
'A Practical Guide to Vicarious Liability' by Mariel Irvine
'A Practical Guide to Applications for Landlord's Consent and Variation of Leases' by Mark Shelton
'A Practical Guide to Relief from Sanctions Post-Mitchell and Denton' by Peter Causton
'A Practical Guide to Equity Release for Advisors' by Paul Sams
'A Practical Guide to Financial Services Claims' by Chris Hegarty

'The Law of Houses in Multiple Occupation: A Practical Guide to HMO Proceedings' by Julian Hunt
'Occupiers, Highways and Defective Premises Claims: A Practical Guide Post-Jackson – 2nd Edition' by Andrew Mckie
'A Practical Guide to Financial Ombudsman Service Claims' by Adam Temple & Robert Scrivenor
'A Practical Guide to Advising Schools on Employment Law' by Jonathan Holden
'A Practical Guide to Running Housing Disrepair and Cavity Wall Claims: 2nd Edition' by Andrew Mckie & Ian Skeate
'A Practical Guide to Holiday Sickness Claims – 2nd Edition' by Andrew Mckie & Ian Skeate
'Arguments and Tactics for Personal Injury and Clinical Negligence Claims' by Dorian Williams
'A Practical Guide to Drone Law' by Rufus Ballaster, Andrew Firman, Eleanor Clot
'A Practical Guide to Compliance for Personal Injury Firms Working With Claims Management Companies' by Paul Bennett
'RTA Allegations of Fraud in a Post-Jackson Era: The Handbook – 2nd Edition' by Andrew Mckie
'RTA Personal Injury Claims: A Practical Guide Post-Jackson' by Andrew Mckie
'On Experts: CPR35 for Lawyers and Experts' by David Boyle
'An Introduction to Personal Injury Law' by David Boyle
'A Practical Guide to Subtle Brain Injury Claims' by Pankaj Madan

These books and more are available to order online direct from the publisher at www.lawbriefpublishing.com, where you can also read free sample chapters. For any queries, contact us on 0844 587 2383 or mail@lawbriefpublishing.com.

Our books are also usually in stock at www.amazon.co.uk with free next day delivery for Prime members, and at good legal bookshops such as Wildy & Sons.

We are regularly launching new books in our series of practical day-to-day practitioners' guides. Visit our website and join our free newsletter to be kept informed and to receive special offers, free chapters, etc.

You can also follow us on Twitter at www.twitter.com/lawbriefpub.

www.ingramcontent.com/pod-product-compliance
Lightning Source LLC
LaVergne TN
LVHW022310200926
848481LV00004B/1266